The Secret Game

A play in two acts

by

Anne Le Marquand Hartigan

CHISWICK BOOKS

LONDON

www.chiswickbooks.com

First published in 2014 by Chiswick Books, 2 Prebend Gardens, Chiswick, London W4 1TW.
www.chiswickbooks.com
info@chiswickbooks.com

The Secret Game © Anne Le Marquand Hartigan 1995

Anne Le Marquand Hartigan is hereby identified as author of this play in accordance with section 77 of the Copyright, Designs and Patents Act 1988. The author has asserted her moral rights.

All rights whatsoever in the play are strictly reserved and application for performance etc. should be made before commencement of rehearsal by email to: rights@annehartigan.ie. No performance may be given unless a licence has been obtained, and no alterations may be made in the title or the text of the play without the author's prior written consent.

This book is sold subject to the condition that it shall not by way of trade or otherwise be circulated without the publisher's consent in any form of binding or cover or circulated electronically other than that in which it is published and without a similar condition including this condition being imposed on any subsequent purchaser.

British Library Cataloguing in Publication Data. A catalogue record for this book is available from the British Library.

This is a work of fiction. Names, characters, places and incidents either are products of the author's imagination or are used fictitiously. Any resemblance to actual events or locales or persons, living or dead, is entirely coincidental.

ISBN:978-0-9928692-0-5

Cover image from a painting by Anne Le Marquand Hartigan.

Also by the author

Plays

Beds, *Chiswick Books, 2016*
I Do Like to be Beside the Seaside, *Chiswick Books, 2016*
Jersey Lilies, *Chiswick Books, 2016*
La Corbière, *Chiswick Books, 2016*
Three Short Plays, *Chiswick Books, 2016*

Poetry

Unsweet Dreams, *Salmon Poetry, 2011*
To Keep The Light Burning, *Salmon, 2008*
Nourishment, *Salmon Poetry, 2005*
Immortal Sins, *Salmon Poetry, 1993*
Now is a Moveable Feast, *Salmon Poetry, 1991*
Return Single, *Beaver Row Press, 1986*
Long Tongue, *Beaver Row Press, 1982*

Prose

Clearing the Space, *Salmon Poetry, 1996*

To Tim and our family, Dominic, Mark, Jerome, Marianne, Elizabeth and Hugh and their spouses Kirsty, Karen, Adriane, Brendan, Tim and Zelda.

Characters

AUNT	*Late sixties/early seventies, bright and young for her age. She has a dog (not seen on stage) that she talks to.*
CHRIS	*Mid thirties, niece to AUNT.*
NOEL	*Late teens, a member of a terrorist organisation.*
CHARLIE	*Late thirties, a member of a terrorist organisation and childhood friend of CHRIS.*

Time and place

The action takes place from one evening through to the early morning, Ireland, just south of the Northern Irish border in the early 1990s.

Set

The main action of the play takes place inside an old barn, now unused for daily farming activities. It houses some bales of silage. The barn belongs to AUNT, whose home is a few hundred yards away down a hill. Front left of the stage is AUNT's home. There are two different places on stage at the same time. (Details of AUNT's place below at the beginning of Act One).

A small car is left of centre stage. Downstage right, there are huge black plastic bales of silage in a pile. Above this, from centre stage to stage right, is a loft with a ladder. This is a simple platform. There is one small window at the loft level. All the set is staged as simply as possible. Lighting is used to create the space outside the barn; and the light is reduced to make the interior claustrophobic. Objects that are particular to the characters are brought up and lit, very subtly, given just slight emphasis at times, e.g. for NOEL: the gun, the walkie-talkie; for CHRIS there are childhood mementoes: a doll etc. The sound of rain continues all through the play from the end of scene one.

Note on the text

The Banshee is a mythical Irish harbinger of death.

Kuryakin is a character from the 1960s TV series, *The Man From U.N.C.L.E,* which CHRIS and CHARLIE would have watched.

Act One

Scene One

The stage is dark, misty. A circle of light comes up on AUNT. She is in her own pool of light as in an old photograph. Her place is stage front left. AUNT is on stage for the whole play. We see, or half-see her, when she is not in the action. She talks to her dog, Bono. Her face is bathed in rosy light as the sun sets. She is looking at a plant outside the door to her garden. A light comes up on the curving plant. She is comfortable in herself. It is peaceful.

AUNT

>Bono. I thought it had had it. Touch and go though. It's grown in such a beautiful curve over that archway, and honeysuckles usually are no trouble. No trouble at all. Then it didn't flower and the leaves went blackish. I kept on spraying it with soap suds. Looked hopeless. It was Chris who told me about the soapy water treatment. To spray the poor plant with buckets of it. Oh the poor thing. Seemed so cruel. But hooray, Bono,

it's done the trick. The lovely thing, all covered with strong new leaves. Look, look, budding up too. Lovely. Soon we will have flowers. This year there will be flowers.

Pause.

A red sky at night is the shepherd's delight.

The sky was lovely and rosy but it's changing rapidly, that harsh yellow and those bluey black clouds, a sure sign of rain. Not good, but we'll hope for good things.

Looks at her dog.

You're right Bono, dinner time. There's a good girl, I'm hungry myself. Come on.

The light on plant fades so AUNT is now inside and feeding the dog. The news is on the radio. Opens a can of dog food.

Chris is coming tonight Bono. You'll like that won't you?

Pause.

Remind me to shut up the geese. Just you remind me. That brindled fox must be rearing her young. Saw her from the upstairs window. Never seen a fox the size of her.

Pause.

Bit worried about Chris, Bono, didn't sound like herself. She's special to me, Bono, really special. *Bends to rub Bono.*

Yes, yes, you're a special girl, you're my special girl, of course you are. We'll have a good long talk with Chris when she comes, won't we? Hot whiskies by the fire and maybe she'll stay two nights. That would be good wouldn't it? There now, sit. Stay.

Puts down the food. Pause.

Go on now.

She watches Bono with satisfaction. Sits and reads the paper, news still murmuring on. Reports of terrorist activity, the border is mentioned.

OK girl, that's it. All gone? Lovely grub! Good girl. Off we go and shut up the geese.

Whistles a tune.

There's rain in the air, Bono my girl, I can smell it. The sunset was lying. I'm afraid I'm right, the red is fading fast. The rain is there. The plants will be happy. So what about it!

Light on her fades.

Fair daffodils we weep to see you haste away so soon...

Light low.

Fade to blackout. Sound of heavy rain in the twilight. Then up slowly to light up as if a lamp in the window is throwing its light on AUNT as she looks out through the window downstage so her face is very visible.

Now it comes. The soft rain, falling, falling. Chris will be here in an hour or so. Sooner maybe. She's a good driver. Rain, rain, rain. At least there's no wind to damage the new leaves, and no frost to burn them.

Light fades to blackout.

Scene Two

Lights up. A spot on CHRIS who is driving her car. We see her head and shoulders and her hands on the wheel. Only her face is clear. We hear the sound of the car engine and windscreen wipers.

CHRIS

Nearly there. Thank God. Made it. I've done it.

Bloody rain. Miserable. I've made it.

Pause.

I've done it.

Pause.

I'm here. Oh my God. Oh God. Why does it rain like that on and on and on? As if it had never rained in its life before. How do we survive this on and on and on?

Pause. Sound only of windscreen wipers and car engine.

I can't wait to get there. I'll put the car straight in the barn. It's nearly over.

Pause.

It's great to have Auntie. She's a Godsend. There's the barn now. The same. Just the same. Always has been a haven. This was our secret place when we were little, Jimmy and I. I can smell its smell. Our plans... what you believe as children, so important at the time. And Charlie... such a bully. How I hated him. Just a little wimp now. How funny. It's not at all funny, it's awful. Just need a few days. A bit of rest.

Pause.

I'll be alright. Maybe I can manage without talking. Don't feel that bad. Considering. Don't consider. All the considering has been done. Finished. It's over. Must let it be over.

Pause.

There's the light on in the kitchen. She'll have put on the electric blanket. Oh I'm so tired. A warm bed, what could be sweeter? Wake up to the sound of birds, and her noisy geese.

Pause.

She won't have heard me. She's a bit deaf. Bono may have heard, but he's getting on too. Dogs hear so much, know so much. I know so little. The gift I need is wisdom. Understanding, fear of the Lord.

Pause. The rain continues. Engine sound continues.

Steady up. Quieten down. It's all OK. Alright. I'll be alright. It's more frightening at night crossing the border. Those babies with guns. Frightening themselves, and us. Lots of soldiers out tonight.

More than usual? What's usual for God's sake!

Car sounds fade, then cease. Wipers fade and then this sound ceases as the lights fade to blackout. Sound of heavy rain.

Scene Three

Lights up on AUNT. She is sitting in her kitchen talking to herself.

AUNT

Rain is comforting. It's good the way the weather controls the world. Just listen to that soft sound. Goodness, it's really pouring, like thunderstorm rain. It's satisfying. Here we are Bono, safe and warm, warm and safe. I might light a fire. That would be nice wouldn't it? You could toast your little belly at it. Be welcoming for Chris too. Hope she takes care in the wet, driving is so tiring in the wet. There is enough turf in so I don't have to go out. Come on then, out with the firelighters and warm ourselves up with a fire. That will be so cosy. Goody goody.

Lights fade on AUNT.

Scene Four

Very dim light comes up, revealing barely discernible large double doors, the inside of the barn. The effect of the large doors is created with light; first dark then lighter as the doors burst open. The rosy, but dimming sunset is alluded to. Sound of heavy rain. Sound of small car driving up outside barn. Sound of it stopping. Sound of the doors bursting open.

Headlights of the car blast into the barn and into the eyes of the audience. Car drives in and stops. In the headlights, the sleeping form of NOEL in a sleeping bag is seen for a moment. He is immediately awoken and leaps up and tackles CHRIS, pulling her out of the car and holding her while he bangs the barn doors shut. CHRIS and NOEL speak across each other.

CHRIS

    Who are you?

NOEL

    What the fuck!

CHRIS

    Christ!

NOEL

>   Get out of it.

CHRIS

>   Let go. Who in the hell are you? What the hell are you doing here?

NOEL

>   Bloody fucking hell, shut up will you?

CHRIS

>   Who are you? What are you doing here? Leave me alone.

NOEL

>   Who are you? Be quiet can't you?

CHRIS

>   What the hell are you doing here?

NOEL

>   Having a kip.

CHRIS

>   I can see that... you scared the life out of me.

NOEL

>   And the shit out of me...

CHRIS

>   What are you doing sleeping here? This is my

aunt's barn. You have no right to be here. Get out at once. Oh, you scared the life out of me. Oh, this is too much. Who are you? What's your name?

NOEL

Couldn't get a lift all evening. Bloody rain. Thought I'd crash out. It's been a cruel day. Not a decent sinner on the road. Walked miles.

CHRIS

Who are you? Tell me your name. Where are you from?

NOEL

Derry.

CHRIS

Where are you heading?

NOEL

To the city.

CHRIS

You'd better get moving so.

NOEL

In that?

Indicates the rain with a jerk of the head.

Have a heart.

CHRIS

That's one thing I'm short of tonight. You've scared the wits out of me. You've no right here. You didn't ask my auntie's permission.

NOEL

Well now, I'm only resting, sheltering from the rain for a wee while, I'm doing no harm. How do you know I didn't ask your auntie?

CHRIS

I just know. On your way young fella.

NOEL

Are you's psychic?

CHRIS

I don't have to be. I know my auntie.

NOEL

So do I. Nice woman.

CHRIS

She is. One of the best. How do you know her?

NOEL

As you say. One of the best.

Pause.

I've been around.

CHRIS

You're too smart for your own good.

NOEL

You might be right or you might not. But you're not hospitable to a man on the road.

CHRIS

Will you shut up and get out of here.

NOEL

You have terrible manners for a good looking woman.

CHRIS

I hate blather.

NOEL

You've your head screwed on. That's a fine car.

CHRIS

There's plenty of traffic on the main road.

NOEL

Mean bastards the lot of them. Always the worst in the wet.

CHRIS

> You'll get a lift. Get going.

NOEL

> I have a better idea, you and me go down to Auntie, and you get a good warm bed for me... No, no, no, no, don't get me wrong. A room for me and a room for you. Say I was hitching and you took pity on me, being the Christian woman you are.
>
> *Silence.*
>
> You look pale.
>
> *He moves closer.*

CHRIS

> Bumping into you hasn't improved my day either. You've one hell of a nerve.
>
> *She moves back and picks up her case.*

NOEL

> Shrinking violets never get anywhere.
>
> *Chris takes the car keys out of her pocket.*
>
> Off on the holidays?

CHRIS

> No one would mistake you for a wallflower. Time for you to hit the road.

NOEL

> I'm a good driver. Tell you what I'll be your chauffeur. Free of charge, you couldn't beat that now.
>
> *CHRIS makes to get into the car again.*
>
> Baby, I couldn't do without you. You're not going to leave me here on my ownio.
>
> *Lights fade.*

Scene Five

Lights come up on scene of AUNT in her chair, classical music is playing.

AUNT

> Tomorrow, Bono, I'll take Chris around the garden and show her where I planted the Lily-of-the-Valley her mother gave me. It will be in flower soon. My mother always gave me a bunch on my birthday. She grew them under the deodar tree. They like the shade, hate sunlight, prefer shady places. White and green, beautiful, pure, each perfect little flower, and scent! Oh scent

from the Garden of Paradise, and they are also - poisonous.

AUNT reacts as if the dog has stood up.

Hear anything Bono? You have to have ears for two now. I'm delighted with the hostas. You listen!

She listens.

No? Nothing. Soon, soon, she'll be here soon. The hostas have had a resurrection from the dead. They had suffered murder by slug. Since I got that tip about putting Vaseline around the pots, the hostas are perfect. I know you don't like them Bono. But they have dramatic leaves and grow in the shade. There's not a bite out of them now. Hostas are Cordon Bleu for slugs. Gourmet dinner for slugs. When I lived in the city, Bono, long before you were born, there were lots of slugs there too. Used to throw the slugs over the wall, into the garden next door. Bad of me. But they did nothing to their garden so it was a haven for slugs. I never put them over the other wall where they cared about their garden.

Moves and looks out the window.

It's a good thing to have a slug haven.

Ecological. That's the "in" word.

Pause.

It's become a desperate night. Desperate.

Light fades down.

Scene Six

Lights up in the barn. CHRIS has put her bag in the car and is on the point of getting in. NOEL is beside her, leaning over her.

NOEL

> Why move the car woman? Didn't you bring it in for the night? Safer, in these parts. Cars get stolen so they do.
>
> *Silence.*
>
> I tell you what, girl, you drop me down the road a bit, on to the main road. What's fairer than that? You're a wee bit tired. But I know you'd like to help a man. You seem a decent woman. Get in there, I'll drive you. You are a bit on the tired side for driving. Sure your hands are shaking. Poor wee thing.

CHRIS pushes NOEL aside, she gets out of the car with her case and walks towards the barn door. NOEL gets in her way.

So it's no lift for me is it? You're a hard-hearted woman. But no matter, I'll walk you down to your auntie. Is she waiting on you with the light in the window there? Or are you surprising her? I think she has a kettle on. I could do with a cup of tea. Does she make a good cup of tea? A woman who doesn't make a good cup of tea is no good to man nor beast.

CHRIS halts in the doorway, not knowing whether to go down to the house or not.

CHRIS

I can walk down on my own thanks. After you.

She stands back to let him pass before her.

You get on your way now and no more of this messing. You should keep off other people's territory, giving them frights. We've enough on our plates. The sooner you get on the road now the quicker you'll get a lift. It's not late yet.

CHRIS moves to go.

NOEL

Here let me.

Goes to take her case.

Let it not be said I'm not a gentleman.

CHRIS

> I'll manage myself.

NOEL

> That's just where you're wrong, lady. Just where you are so wrong. None of us can manage very much by ourselves. Ah, isn't that your auntie by the window? She's looking out for you. Come on girl. Don't keep her waiting.

As CHRIS moves to go he tries to take the case from her. She resists. He holds her.

CHRIS

> *Struggling.*
>
> Take your hands off me, leave me be, let me alone.

NOEL

> *Sings:*
>
> Sweetheart, Sweetheart, Sweetheart,
>
> *Says:*
>
> Sorry about this love. I'm not hitching anywhere tonight. And you're not going anywhere tonight unless I say so. You just keep quiet darling, and

no harm will come to you...

Pause.

...I hope. Just be a good girl.

Pause.

Now darling, tell me where you've come from today, and why you're visiting your auntie tonight and not driving back to Dublin to your husband? Nice rings he's given you. Nice.

CHRIS

Listen, young fella, I have to get down to my aunt now. There's no point in this, this is nothing to do with me, I need to... you don't understand. What's the game? I'm no use to you.

NOEL

You're right, you're no use. Just trouble.

CHRIS turns to leave. NOEL pulls a gun. Puts it in CHRIS's back. She faces the audience, the gun in her back.

Stop. Shut up. No noise.

CHRIS stops. Is silent.

Don't open your mouth. Feel this in your back darling. It's the real thing. This can go off. And you wouldn't feel the better for it. It makes a bit of a mess when it goes off, so it does. I'd prefer not to have to use it, really I would.

Light fades down on CHRIS and NOEL.

Scene Seven

Spot up on AUNT. The news is heard on the radio indistinctly in the background.

AUNT

> *Speaking her thoughts aloud as she writes to her brother Kevin.*

I will try and finish this letter to you before Chris arrives. She is due any time now. I had a good day in the garden. The weather kept up well and I was able to tackle some of the weeds. But now the rain has come in and seems set in for the night. Chris is driving down from Belfast. She has an old school friend living there. She'll stay the night with me and head back to Dublin tomorrow, no doubt. She always does too much. These young mothers have so much on their plates. There's a lot to be said for staying single, Kevin. I don't think Chris has been too well lately, though she laughs it off - you know her way - and says she's fine. Stubborn. I can just hear you saying you know where she gets that from. Keep her in your prayers at Mass, Kevin.

Pause.

AUNT gets up and moves to window and looks out.

Did you hear that Bono? Are you going deaf too or what? I heard something. Was it the fox or the owls?

She listens. Just the sound of the rain.

I think it was the fox...

Lights down on AUNT.

Scene Eight

Lights up in the barn. CHRIS sits on the plastic covered bales. NOEL sits opposite her holding the gun nonchalantly.

NOEL

>Not part of the scenery, honey. You're just not part of the scenery. Pretty. Could say that. Birds

look good in nests. Should stay there. Fly out in their pretty feathers. Get shot. Bang, bang, bang. Pity. Should stay at home. Minding the babbies. That's the place for them. Keep their little beaks out of trouble. Oh dear, yes. Too few brains in the little birds' heads. Such a pity they can't keep their pretty little noses out of other people's business.

Pause.

Let's get things straight, baby.

CHRIS

I'm not your baby - or anyone's baby. No fucking babies. Right!

NOEL

No filthy language, woman.

CHRIS

You can kill me can't you? Stupid little eejit. With you're stupid little gun. Big boy.

NOEL

You keep that mouth of yours shut.

Silence.

CHRIS

Shoot, if you want to. Shoot me. Another life

taken. I'm nothing. OK? I'm nothing. Baby!
What age are you? Eighteen? Nineteen? Twenty?
Oh, you're so big. Oh, you'll solve the world.
I'm sick of you. I'm sick of it. I'll huff and I'll
puff and I'll blow your house in. Murder. Murder.
Murder.

NOEL grabs her.

NOEL

> You just shut up.

CHRIS

> I won't shut up. Kill me and I'll shut up... I don't care, what do I care?

NOEL

> I can make you shut up. I can do what I like with you.
>
> *Silence.*
>
> Man to woman.
>
> *He moves and is standing over her.*
>
> I can, can't I? I can take you any way I want but that's not our way. We have our principles. I'm a man of principle. I don't take advantage of women. This gun speaks a pure language. You

know where you are with a gun. Cool, clean, true.
I am a pure man. I know what truth is.

CHRIS

You know nothing. Nothing of life. You're a
taker. Destroyer. Only able to act with the power
of the bullet. You have the gun, I have the gun.
So bloody what? You only hold death in your
hand. Only death.

NOEL

You haven't met death yet, baby. I've met death
quite often for a young fella. Not always a pretty
face either.

CHRIS

Life's face is not pretty.

NOEL

Life's a bitch

CHRIS

We only get one shot at it.

NOEL

Say that again, baby.

CHRIS

Don't call me baby...

A bleep from a walkie-talkie is heard.

NOEL

> Silence!
>
> *NOEL speaks into a walkie-talkie keeping watch on CHRIS. CHRIS jumps up and runs, scrambles over the silage bags, falls.*

Scene Nine

Light up on AUNT who is cooking.

AUNT

> Keep your ears cocked for the car, Bono, I rely on your good ears. You'll have the bone, never fear. Good stock - good soup. Lovely fresh herbs from the garden. Leeks, potatoes, onions, garlic. Plenty of garlic. Garlic for health. Garlic for healing. For colds. No, no, no, no, not for you, Bono. No, no, just the bone, with some marrow left. Just for you. Don't worry I won't forget you. Parsley, marjoram. Soup for comfort, soup for warmth. Warmth, healing warmth. There now, patience Bono, there's the girl, we all need

patience. Even little dogs. There you are at last, the bone. *Throws the dog the bone.*

Enjoy that, every last bit of it.

Lights down on AUNT.

Scene Ten

Lights up on barn. CHRIS is tied. Silence.

CHRIS

> I insist you let me go down to the house. You'll regret it if you don't.
>
> *Silence. NOEL listens on the walkie-talkie.*
>
> I can't stay here. My aunt is expecting me she'll phone the guards if I don't arrive.
>
> *NOEL still listens.*
>
> I expect she phoned already. She's no fool.

NOEL

> A foolish woman. That's what she'd be, a foolish woman. I hope for your sake she is not that foolish.
>
> *NOEL stands beside CHRIS looking down.*

Blood?

CHRIS

Blood. Yes. It happens to us. It's part of us.

NOEL

Do something about it.

CHRIS

You do something.

Pause.

What can I do, tied like this?

NOEL

Bloody woman.

CHRIS

You're right for once.

NOEL

You've too much cheek in you. You need a lesson. Clean yourself. It's... disgusting

CHRIS

You should be able for blood. You're steeped in it. Up to the bloody elbows in it. My blood is good. Clean.

NOEL

Stand. Stand can't you.

CHRIS

>   What a gallant gentleman. Bring my bag to me.

NOEL

>   For what?

CHRIS

>   For this.
>
>   *Looks down at the blood staining her clothes.*
>
>   So I can look after myself.

NOEL

>   You can stay in it.

CHRIS

>   Pig.

NOEL

>   Watch it. I'll tape your mouth.
>
>   *Silence.*

CHRIS

>   You're a fine example of a civilised man. Ireland should be proud of you, her son. How glad I am I've met you.
>
>   *Bleep from the walkie-talkie. It appears orders are being issued to NOEL. He walks away from CHRIS to listen, keeping an eye on her, gun at*

the ready. Conversation ends. Goes to small window up the ladder and watches. Comes down. Opens barn door slightly. watches. CHRIS follows him with her eyes. He goes to the car and gets her bag. Flings it down beside her. Pulls her to her feet and cuts the ties.

NOEL

>Tidy yourself up, woman.
>
>*He moves back to the barn door, keeps gun on CHRIS. She walks to the car carrying her bag. Lights down. Blackout.*

Scene Eleven

The barn, later. CHRIS is bound again. NOEL sits with her bag. He is taking things out of it. They sit on the silage bales. NOEL takes things out slowly. Sometimes he chuckles.

NOEL

>Before I gag you. I need to see what you have in this bag of yours. Need to ask a few questions you know? Just to see you're bone fide, you know what I mean? Have to do a check-up.

Mostly wasting my time but you never know, you might be helpful after all. I know you'd love to be helpful, seems to be your nature doesn't it, honey?

Pause.

Not speaking are we? Well, well. You will sweetie. Dressing gown. Nighty. *Two* nighties. What's that? Blood on the nighty? Pants, a bra. Where were you staying love? And how long for? Washbag, hairbrush, make-up bag. Would you like to put on your face? You look a bit… Let's look at you… Not your best, I think. Age showing tonight. Don't I turn you on? I'm good in the sack, baby.

Licks up the side of CHRIS's face. CHRIS recoils.

CHRIS

Get away from me. You're disgusting.

NOEL

Must get on with the work. Pleasure later. Handbag. Tells you a lot about a woman, a handbag does. Wallet. Photos. Ah, the children, and the lovely husband. All so well, so happy.

Snaps.

Names?

CHRIS

> John

NOEL

> John who?

CHRIS

> Quinn.

NOEL

> *Snaps.*
>
> Age? And occupation?

CHRIS

> Thirty nine, a civil servant.

NOEL

> And the childer, name and age?

CHRIS

> Christopher, ten; Jessica, six; Mary Louise, three.

NOEL

> They are lovely kids, especially the baby, God bless 'em. Take good care of them. Where have you been up north? When did you go? Where did you stay, and why?

CHRIS

> I stayed with Pauline Long in Belfast, two nights. We were at school together.

NOEL

> Why?

CHRIS

> We like each other. We are friends. I go up now and again, she comes down to me. It makes a break, we do some shopping and talk and things. See a show or that sort of thing.

NOEL

> How nice. How pally. When did you last go?

CHRIS

> Ages ago, I can't remember.

NOEL

> Why?

CHRIS

> Why should I?

NOEL

> You just should, baby.

CHRIS

>   Oh, I think she came to me last time. Before
>   Christmas, to go shopping and to the panto.

NOEL

>   Sweet. Sweet. And what's the address of nice
>   little friend Pauline? You haven't told me that.
>   Or if she has a husband, and his name? And what
>   does he do in a line of business? Come on, come
>   on, no messing.

CHRIS

>   Pauline and Robert Johnson live in Hollywood.

NOEL

>   Yes?

CHRIS

>   23 Crescent Terrace.

NOEL

>   Oh, nice. Well for them.

CHRIS

>   Robert works at Queen's. He's American. She has
>   just been made redundant.

NOEL

>   And what do you work at? Or do you just go

gallivanting around pleasing yourself? Besides being a housewife. Or are you just a housewife?

CHRIS

I am a secretary, part-time. For the moment.

NOEL has been looking amongst CHRIS's papers and finds, among other things, her passport.

NOEL

A woman should mind her children. Interesting. Don't need this up north.

Indicating her passport.

CHRIS

Helpful to carry it. I always do when I travel.

NOEL

Is it helping you? Oh, I say, that photo doesn't do you justice. Made a balls of that, they did. Didn't help you with the names they gave you, your parents, did they? Christine, Mabel, Gertrude. God in heaven. What a lot to be dumped with.

Pause.

Explain this ticket.

Silence.

A return flight from Belfast to London. You

went two days ago and back this evening. Friend Pauline go with you? Or, a man, maybe?

Silence.

No point in not speaking, sweetheart. Just no point at all.

CHRIS

Yes, she did. Pauline and I went together.

NOEL

Another little shopping trip?

CHRIS

Well. Yes. That's right.

NOEL

Didn't buy much, did you?

CHRIS

There are things in the boot

NOEL

There is nothing in the boot.

CHRIS

Pauline must have forgotten to put them back. It's dangerous to leave anything in your car in Belfast, as you know. Are they really not in the boot? I had presents for the children.

NOEL

> Quick talking, baby.
>
> *A vixen's cry is heard.*
>
> What was that?

CHRIS

> The Banshee.

NOEL

> It was a dog

CHRIS

> No. It was not.

NOEL

> No more from you. No one believes in the Banshee any more.

CHRIS

> They do.

NOEL

> Who's heard it?

CHRIS

> I have. And others.

NOEL

> Who? Who do you know has heard it?

CHRIS

> My aunt.

NOEL

> You're only women. What were you doing in the UK?

CHRIS

> We shopped. We saw shows. Had fun.

NOEL

> Where did you stay?

CHRIS

> With a friend.

NOEL

> Address?

CHRIS

> We stayed… Oh I'm not good at remembering addresses. She was a friend of Pauline's in Hampstead, 14a was the number, Throttle Street, I think. We took tubes and taxis. I just went along, Pauline did the arranging.

NOEL

> Expect me to swallow that, baby?
> Put your head up and look at me.

CHRIS

>	I don't feel well. I'm dizzy.

NOEL

>	Liars never feel well. Bad liars like you feel worse.

CHRIS

>	Look who's talking.
>
>	*CHRIS faints. NOEL doesn't know what to do. Then tries to help revive CHRIS. She comes out of her faint.*

NOEL

>	What's up with you woman?

CHRIS

>	I'm alright, I'll be better in a moment.

NOEL

>	Do you do that often?

CHRIS

>	What?

NOEL

>	Faint.

CHRIS

>	No. But...

NOEL

> What's up with you?

CHRIS

> Nothing. I must go down to the house. Let me go down to the house.
>
> *A Garda (police) car siren is heard.*

NOEL

> Do you think I'm a fool? Have sense.

CHRIS

> I just need sleep, that's all I need.

NOEL

> There's more blood on you. Can you not look after yourself? I've never met a woman like you.

CHRIS

> You know nothing about women.

NOEL

> I do so, I've sisters.

CHRIS

> God help them. Please let me out of here, I'm no good to you.

NOEL

> I know that.

Pause.

You're no good. You're right there. Dead right. What were you up to in England?

CHRIS

I've told you.

NOEL

Have you now? I think you've told me a ball of lies.

CHRIS

It must be lovely to lie easily like you. No bother to you at all.

NOEL

Did your husband, Johnny boy, know you were going on this wee outing?

Silence.

I bet he didn't. I bet he's in the dark about it all. Poor little sod. While his wee wifey is gallivanting all over the place.

CHRIS

I have no secrets from John. Nor he from me. Have you got someone special in your life? A girlfriend?

NOEL

> My life is my business. You're just no good, that's what. You've come back from England and I know why you went. You didn't go for any good time, you went there to commit an evil deed. You're an evil woman. I thought you were a decent woman. That's a filthy act you've done. I have no pity for you. You'll destroy civilisation so you will. Women like you are scum. What are you up to? You with a husband and children and money. You're fine. You're a queen bee. You've got it easy. Selfish, dead selfish. I know what you've done. You've got rid of a child. A totally innocent child. You've killed a child, that's what you've done. You've killed a helpless innocent. I hate the likes of you. A murdering woman is an abomination.

CHRIS

You little arsehole. You little shit. You know nothing. You kill because Big Boss tells you. You wipe out and run. Murder is everyday to you. You're so stupid. You will be wiped out. All you make is death, scars and pain. You breed death.

NOEL

> Just don't you call me stupid. I warn you, don't you ever say that again or you'll be sorry. Shut up, and don't you preach to me woman. You're the one who's committed a crime, against the whole of mankind.

CHRIS

> Mankind. Mankind. What about womankind? You know nothing about me. You can't judge me. It's my body, I make my decisions about it. I make my decisions about my life. I've risked birth, no man does that. But how you love to play with death. Others' deaths. I have no time for you. I take my decisions for life. Love hurts. Making life brings pain. Some decisions are terrible. But, I have discovered that there are things I have to be true to, no matter what. You can kill me. So easy for you. Where will that get you?

NOEL

> You're true to nothing. You're a cheating hoor. Some bastard's baby in you. Had to get away quick before your husband found out. You're a slut, that's what you are. A dirty slut. Woman like you destroy the honour of the world.

CHRIS

> Honour! Why do I bother to speak with you? You don't know a thing. You know nothing. You know nothing of me, I won't defend myself to you. Why should I? You may have had to make decisions that tear you apart. But I doubt it, you are so cock-sure. So certain. You sicken me.

NOEL

> Cunt.
>
> *NOEL spits on the floor. Three taps on the door. Blackout.*

Scene Twelve

Light comes up quickly on AUNT who is on the phone.

AUNT

> It's early in the year. Not much of a show I'm afraid yet... Yes. I'll let you have some for the sale of work. Of course I will. I'd be very pleased... I'll do it when I'm dividing the daffodils. I need to divide the daffodils this year, they are ready for it. Will do them good.
>
> *Listens.*

My niece is fine, Father, works too hard, not as easy as it was when I was young...The children are fine... Yes, he's fine... I haven't seen her for a while now... Please God... Yes, please God, we will. We could do with a spot of warmth. The sun does us all a power of good. Brings out the best in us. Plants and people all respond to a bit of sun... Grand Father... Yes... Yes... Bye now... Bye.

Replaces the receiver. Listens.

It is a fox. Is it a fox Bono? Oh I wish I could hear as I did. Mind you it has its advantages, I can't hear Father Kirk's boring sermons even if I wanted to. Can have a little zizz. Listen, there it is again! Don't you hear it you silly dog?

Pause.

I don't like that. It reminds me of the Banshee.

Pause.

Chris is taking longer than I'd like... Should have been here by now. There it is again, that howl. You must have heard it, Bono.

Pause. Blackout.

Scene Thirteen

Lights up on the barn.

NOEL

> Listen and be quiet. There is waiting to do. I have work to do. Soon I will tape your mouth and blindfold your eyes. I advise you to make no protest or I will have to shoot you. Your fate will be decided later. Now, we will wait.
>
> *Silence.*
>
> Have you questions?
>
> *Silence.*
>
> Why do you say nothing?

CHRIS

> I have nothing to say. I have nothing to say to you. I need my bag. Give me my bag.

NOEL

> Please?
>
> *Pause.*
>
> Your manners are atrocious. Who reared you?
>
> *Pause.*

CHRIS

> Please.

NOEL

> You can do better than that.
>
> *Pause.*

CHRIS

> Please can I have my bag?

NOEL

> Good girl. You're coming on. What do you want from it?

CHRIS

> Codeine.

NOEL

> What's that?

CHRIS

> Like Aspro, for pain, for headache.

NOEL

> These them?
>
> *Holds up a bottle*

CHRIS

> Yes.

NOEL

> *Shakes out pills into his hand.*
>
> Here's three for you, that's enough.

CHRIS

> That will do.
>
> *She takes them. NOEL pulls a flask from CHRIS's bag and gives her a cup of cold tea. He sits beside CHRIS. CHRIS keeps apart from him as much as possible. Silence.*

NOEL

> Where are you from?
>
> *Silence.*
>
> We have time to kill, why not make the best of it?

CHRIS

> If that was all you killed.

NOEL

> What's that?

CHRIS

> Time.

NOEL

> Speak for yourself woman. Watch it.

CHRIS

> Can you kill time as well, clever boy?

NOEL

> No lip from you, woman. Mind that tongue of yours.
>
> *Silence.*
>
> Do you play cards?
>
> *No response.*
>
> Have it your own way.
>
> *Takes out a pack and begins to play cards on the floor. Soft light up on AUNT who is seen playing patience. She has music playing. After a short while NOEL hums or whistles the same tune. Light fades to blackout on AUNT and music fades. NOEL continues to hum.*
>
> Did you play here as kids?

CHRIS

> Why do you want to know? Why should I tell you anything?
>
> *Pause.*

NOEL

> You don't need to get so shirty. I haven't touched

you. I have a job to do that's all, but tell me anyway?

CHRIS

We did, my brother and I. My brother Jimmy and I. We played here.

Pause.

And Charlie.

NOEL

I have a brother, Jim, in England. Wife and kids. Works at the building. His wife's a Chink, you know, Chinese.

Pause.

I could murder a takeaway.

CHRIS

Is that all your family?

NOEL

Enough for you to know about. Before the kids came, they came home to my mother every year for Christmas.

Silence.

CHRIS

What's your name?

NOEL

> *Shrugs.*

> Call me Noel.

CHRIS

> The name's too good for you.

NOEL

> Careful now.

CHRIS

> Your poor mother.

NOEL

> Leave my mother out of it.

CHRIS

> *Talking to herself while NOEL plays cards.*

> A safe place. So near and so far from everything. A secret place. Ours. Barn, barn, save me. Where have the kind spirits of the world gone? You bats up there. The owl. Where are you? Rain washing and washing, wash this away. My blood, my good blood. We had our secrets here, Jimmy, you and I. We shut out the others. Charlie barged his way in. But you liked him. We shut the world out. We planned. We were in touch with space creatures. The aliens were danger. Sky divers from the loft.

I left my little doll. We had a funeral. I wanted to make her alive again but Jimmy and Charlie said I'd be a sissy. I wanted to be a sissy.

Pause.

I didn't get her back.

Scene Fourteen

Childhood

This is played by the actors as if they were children. They do not change their appearance in any way, just assume their childish personalities.

Enter CHARLIE up in the loft. CHRIS goes to the foot of the ladder to the loft. CHRIS and CHARLIE speak to and interact with CHRIS's brother Jimmy, apparently visible to them but there is no one present. NOEL continues for a short time to play cards. He continues in the present while the rest are in a childhood past. So we have two eras on stage at once. A subtle light change marks the move into the past. CHARLIE appears in the loft. He is a child of about ten or eleven. CHRIS, at the foot of the ladder, is about eight or nine years old. She holds her doll. NOEL plays cards, or he continues in the present time interweaving his movements and stillness so the two times work a kind of harmony and the audience is aware of both. He is capable of being very still.

NOEL continues to play cards. CHARLIE is playing as if with Jimmy in the loft.

CHRIS

Can I come up?

Silence.

Can I? Can I come up now?

CHARLIE

No.

CHARLIE squats and is busy with things on the floor of the loft as if with Jimmy.

CHRIS.

Please.

CHARLIE

You keep watch. We need you to keep watch.

Pause.

CHRIS

>	I always keep watch. Keeping watch is boring.

CHARLIE

>	Girls are good at it.
>
>	*Pause.*

CHRIS

>	You never keep watch.
>
>	*Pause.*
>
>	I'm bored of keeping watch.
>
>	*Pause.*
>
>	Can I come up? Now?

CHARLIE

>	No. Jimmy says no.

CHRIS

>	Please? Jimmy, please, can I come up?
>
>	Please?
>
>	*Silence.*
>
>	I'm going home.

CHARLIE

>	Hold on a minute. Nearly ready. We're just
>	putting away all our secret stuff. Then you can

come up. OK Jimmy, there you are. OK boss. Not a word.

CHARLIE crosses the loft and looks out the window. CHARLIE speaks to CHRIS.

We're ready now. It's safe for you to come up now.

CHRIS

I don't think I'm going to play this game any more.

CHARLIE

We're just getting to the really exciting part. We've just heard the aliens making signals. Jimmy picked them up on his receiver. Shhh. Quiet.

A dog barks.

There.

CHRIS

That was Bach.

CHARLIE

Girls know nothing. Aliens disguise themselves as anything.

CHRIS

Bach is an alien? He's just Auntie's dog. He only

>knows dog language. And a bit of ours too.

CHARLIE

>Dogs are very intelligent.

CHRIS

>I'm going. Bach is more fun to play with.

CHARLIE

>You can come up now. We're ready now.

CHRIS

>Oh alright.
>
>*She goes up the ladder.*

CHARLIE

>What a stupid name for a dog. Bark.

CHRIS

>He says his own name, so he is clever. But it's not the word you think.

CHARLIE

>Oh yes it is.

CHRIS

>No it's not. But I won't tell you.

CHARLIE

>What is it then?

CHRIS

> It's the name of a composer who writes music Auntie plays. She's teaching me a tune Bach wrote.

CHARLIE

> It's a stupid old name. The aliens have got him.

CHRIS

> Auntie says his Bach is worse than his bite. She thinks that's funny.

CHARLIE

> It's stupid to call a dog Bark.
>
> *Pause.*
>
> Quiet. Dead quiet. The aliens are outside the door. Have you put our invisible guard on the door, Jimmy?
>
> *Pause.*
>
> Ok, I will.
>
> *Creeps to the window. Makes as if to shoot.*
>
> Pow, pow. Got one with my laser. Got it! That was a great shot I did. Good shot, Jimmy. That's them dealt with for the moment.

CHRIS

At the window.

Pow pow. Got one. Got two.

CHARLIE

No you didn't. You don't have the power, only Jimmy and I have the power.

CHRIS

I do so have the power.

CHARLIE

Girls don't. Do they Jimmy? See, they don't.

CHRIS

I'm fed up with this game. I'm going home.

CHARLIE

Spoilsport.

CHRIS

I'm not.

CHARLIE

Yes, you are. Yes, you are.

CHRIS

You're not fair. I never get a turn at the good things.

CHARLIE

>We are fair. We're older than you so it's fair.
>
>*CHRIS goes down the ladder carefully, one foot at a time, she's a little scared.*

CHRIS

>You're a pig!

CHARLIE

>Hey, don't you call me a pig.
>
>*CHARLIE bounds down the ladder and shoves CHRIS to the side.*
>
>I'm going to play football, come on Jimmy.

CHRIS

>I'm tired. I don't want to play any more.
>
>*She goes and plays with her doll.*

CHARLIE

>Spoilsport. Cry baby.

CHRIS

>I'm not crying.

CHARLIE

>Only sissies play with dolls.
>
>*Silence.*
>
>You're a sissy.

CHRIS

>I'm not. I'm not.

CHARLIE

>You are, you are, you are.
>
>*CHRIS attacks him.*
>
>Hey. Stop it.
>
>*He holds her off.*
>
>I don't fight girls. I'm going to practise football. Coming Jimmy?
>
>*Exit CHARLIE. CHRIS sticks out her tongue when he has gone. She plays with her doll. Sound from outside of CHARLIE kicking the ball.*

CHRIS

>I'm not a sissy, am I, Jimmy? Why can't boys be sissies? Sometimes I think they *are* sissies, don't you? I like football too. Susie has got a headache. That's why I'm minding her. Maybe she's teething. She's dribbling a lot. I think she needs a nice sleep. She needs a rest, I think. It's more fun when Charlie isn't here. I like playing with you. Look, here's the secret message for that friendly alien. I kept it hidden like you said. OK. I'll do it. You mind Susie. Alright don't, if you

don't want to. She'll be alright. I'll just tuck her up first. There, there love, you're a good girl.

CHRIS tucks up doll and climbs up the ladder, goes to the window. Makes signals. Opens window and throws out a note.

He's got it Jimmy. He's got it. He gave a big grin.

She gives Jimmy a thumbs-up sign. Light half up on AUNT, her back half-turned to the audience.

AUNT

Calls:

Jimmy, Chris, Charlie, time for tea! Teatime. Jimmy, Chris, come in for your tea!

They'll be famished as always.

Calls:

Come on now. Don't let it get cold. Chris, Jimmy, Charlie. Teatime!

Light down on AUNT. Enter CHARLIE.

CHRIS

From the loft.

That's Auntie calling. Oh, I'm starving.

CHARLIE

Come on, let's eat. I could eat a mountain.

CHRIS

>I could eat a house.

>*CHARLIE picks up CHRIS's doll and flings her into the back of the barn.*

>Don't. You'll hurt her. Don't!

CHARLIE

>Dolls are stupid. It's thick to like dolls. You can't hurt dolls. Let's go.

>*CHARLIE pulls the ladder back from the loft, he can just manage it.*

>Now you can't get down.

CHRIS

>Put it back, put it back.

CHARLIE

>*Struggling to hold the ladder.*

>Ask nicely.

CHRIS

>Please, Charlie, please!

CHARLIE

>OK.

>*CHARLIE puts back the ladder and runs out.*

CHRIS

> *Coming down the ladder.*
>
> Jimmy. Wait for me Jimmy. Please wait, wait.
>
> *Sound of shutting doors. It gets dark.*
>
> Oh don't shut me in! Please don't shut me in.
> Jimmy, don't let Charlie shut me in.
>
> *CHARLIE's laughter is heard from outside.*
>
> I hate the dark.
>
> *She climbs down the ladder, slowly and carefully.*

CHARLIE

> *From outside.*
>
> You're a sissy, sissy, sissy. Only babies are afraid of the dark.
>
> *CHRIS turns to run out after them.*

CHRIS

> Wait for me. Wait for me. You never wait for me. Don't shut me in. Wait for me!
>
> *Light changes from childhood dream scene. Blackout.*

Act Two

Scene One

In the dark NOEL sings 'My Lagan Love' gently. Lights come up low. NOEL receives information on his walkie-talkie. He watches from the window and by the door. CHRIS is face down, bound and gagged, lying across two seats of the car. Only her legs are visible.

Silently, the barn door opens. A masked figure appears. Torchlight flashes around. NOEL and the masked man split a plastic silage bag open and remove hidden guns and carry them out. This is done with efficiency and speed. Not a word is exchanged. CHRIS does not move nor is she seen by the newcomer. The job is completed and the masked man goes. NOEL tidies the remaining silage bags. The light fades to near blackout. Moves seamlessly into the next scene.

Scene Two

Light up on AUNT. She is putting her letter to Kevin in an envelope.

AUNT

> Every month I do this, write Kevin a letter.
>
> *Pause.*
>
> I don't say what I really feel. I don't know what Kevin feels. His whole life in the priesthood. So far away from all of us. When he comes home he's so - so jolly.
>
> *Pause.*
>
> He always was great fun. Good sense of humour. He and I were the clowns in the family. But now, this jolliness of his is a wall. He keeps behind his wall. He doesn't want to penetrate it. Or me to penetrate it.
>
> *Pause.*
>
> His wall dropped a little when Mother died. Since then it has become thicker.
>
> *Pause.*
>
> I wish he'd stop being jolly. Makes me angry

sometimes, his jokes. He monopolises all the jolliness. Leaves no space for me to be fun. Bother him. Why give it a thought?

Pause.

There is only so much space in a family, you have to claim your bit. He leaves me the sensible space. That's a bore. I think you and I, Bono, will have to plan something distinctly unsensible.

Silence.

We never have a good talk. If I think about it, did we ever have a good talk? Mother having him so late, of course he was her pet. There is a lot to be said for dogs, Bono. You always listen. Except when you're asleep. And you, you perfect creature, you don't even snore.

Pause.

We always want more talk than men.

Pause.

They put everything into sex. What does Kevin do with his sex? I can't ask that in a letter can I, Bono? You think I can? I think you're wrong, because he'd just ignore me and never answer. I'll ask him when he's home again.

Pause.

Bet I don't, I'll chicken out. Would have to be drunk. Might be a good idea. To get drunk together. We never have.

Pause.

What does he think I do with my sex? Does he think I haven't got any? Goodness. I expect he does. Since I was widowed, does he think I have switched off, like a light? Click. Bet he thinks just that. Goodness.

Silence.

What makes me think he thinks about me at all? Except once a month when he gets my boring letter.

Silence.

Tell you what, Bono, would you mind an awful lot if I had a little cat?

Pause.

If we got a kitten you'd help me mind her wouldn't you? We might both enjoy a kitten.

Cross fade from AUNT to CHRIS in barn.

Scene Three

CHRIS is lying against the bags of silage, still bound and gagged. NOEL moves around the barn cat-like and with confidence, up and down, on both levels, checking the windows and the barn door. He is putting everything back as before and finds an old rag doll.

NOEL

>*To himself.*
>
>Done. OK. On their way. Fine. Better that's over. Waiting's the worst. Fucking worst. More waiting. Shit, shit. I've had enough waiting. Her. No problem. I get the drift. That was a good lot. Won't be here again. This is not the worst. This is a fair kip except... Still, shit, shit, shit.
>
>*NOEL takes the gag off CHRIS. Throws down the rag doll in front of her. Sits with back to CHRIS*

CHRIS

>*To herself.*
>
>I need to be with John. I need to be with them, I need them and they need me, we need each other.
>*Pause.*
>
>That was the most difficult birth I have ever

given.

Pause.

I wanted to do nothing. If only I could have gone to sleep and woken up and found everything different. It would have been easy to do nothing.

Pause.

And terrible to do nothing. Agony.

Pause.

Leave decisions to others. Faith without doubting. They know best. Mother knows best, Father knows best. God knows best. God knows everything, lucky old God. Who is God if not that voice in my gut? Everyone knows best. Not me. Do as you are told, tow the line. When they passed them along to the gas chambers they were only obeying orders. Not their fault no, no, no, obey. Then you're good, and we like you. Leave choices to others. To those who know best. Never yourself. Never trust. Never follow your gut, or your intelligence, or your sanity. I'm a chattle, a pudding basin, a hold-all. Go on spewing out, never mind those here, never mind the children I have.

Pause.

I do mind the children, that's what I do. Oh I mind them so much, I love them so much, it's frightening how much I love my children. 'Offer it up,' they said. We were told to offer it up. Self sacrifice. This is my sacrifice of self. This is my body. This is my blood.

Silence.

Lucky doll. Dolls don't feel. Little dolls. We are all your little dolls. Dolly birds. So sweet, tweet, tweet, tweet.

Silence.

My doll. Poor little doll.

Pause.

So stupid and helpless like this. No legs. No arms. No control. Just like you doll. Poor old us. A funny pair we make. Together after all these years. Finding my first love again. It was simple loving you. Simple at the start. Mothers and dolls. There for us. If we're lucky. You look worm-eaten. I'm not that yet anyway. You lie where you're put. What a comfort you were to me. I could hug and cuddle you. Drop you in a corner and you couldn't complain. You were there for me. I didn't need to be there for you.

Pause.

Tied like this, I'm a bit like you. Dumped. We dump cats, dogs, put them down. He tapes my mouth. I'm silenced. You never had a voice, I spoke for you. I knew what you thought and what you would say. You were real. Really real.

Pause.

You've survived all these years, little doll. Will I survive this night? Will I, little Susie? Oh, will I?

Silence.

To NOEL.

And you found her. Where did you find her?

NOEL

At the back there, when moving the... things... found it...

CHRIS

She's so old, so manky, I couldn't find her. We used the shoe box for her coffin. Said prayers too. The boys dug a hole to put the coffin in but I didn't really want her to go down in the hole. So I stopped them, then Charlie grabbed her and threw her somewhere away amongst pitch forks and bales and said dolls were stupid. I cried

and he laughed and Jimmy didn't do anything
because he didn't want to look a sissy in front of
Charlie... You're shaking.

Pause.

Are you cold?

Pause.

Are you ill?

Pause.

NOEL

No. I'm fine. Keep away, woman.

CHRIS

You don't seem fine.

NOEL

Leave me be.

Silence.

I get taken like this.

CHRIS

You're not right, are you?

NOEL

It will pass.

CHRIS

They say all things pass. Or come to pass. I don't

think I believe them.

NOEL

Give us a break.

He shakes. Sound of heavy rain. Cross fade to AUNT.

Scene Four

Light up on AUNT.

AUNT

The silence at this time of night is always the deepest. Sometimes velvety, like sleep itself, but tonight it's hard. I don't like it.

Pause.

Chris is very late and I am not happy. Not at all happy...

Pause.

for her to be late. I expect... rain, road blocks, can be anything. One is always happier if people travel by day but, if the truth be told, you are just as likely to be held up then as in the night.

Pause.

She has not phoned, that's a worrying thing.

Pause.

Bono, Bono, I'll let you out now for your pee. Come on girl, take your little fat belly away from the fire and I'll put you out for a few minutes.

Pause.

I want to talk to Chris, I feel there is a need to talk. She didn't tell me much about this visit. She said enough for me to catch that there was something she wasn't telling me. Oh bloody hell. She had trouble after little Louise. What was it exactly? She didn't tell me much, brushed it off but I expect that was because I was having my hip done. Didn't want to worry me. I'm a bloody fool. I should have remembered to find out from her later. I'll try and talk to John next time if Chris won't say. Be nice if she could stay a day or two. Wouldn't that be lovely Bono? I'll ask her straight out. I think she wants to talk. You have to be so careful and not interfere.

Pause.

What is happening in this night, and what has happened, and what will become of all of us? Bono, come in now, you've had long enough.

What are you barking at, you silly old thing? Will you just stop that. It's too late and dark for that sort of carry-on. Stand still while I dry you. Good little girl. Now. Let's cheer ourselves up with some really cheerful music.

Puts on a CD.

There, that will do us good.

I wonder whether to phone? John? The Guards? What would be best? Bono? What's best?

Puts hand out on to the telephone receiver. Lights fade on AUNT, cross fade to barn.

Scene Five

NOEL sits beside CHRIS. He is shaking. Sound of continuous heavy rain.

NOEL

>What was that?

CHRIS

>Look, a little bat, and there's another.

NOEL

>Dirty things. I hate them. Get in your hair.

CHRIS

> Nonsense. They're fine, this is their home. That's an old husbands' tale. And the owls. The owls live here.

NOEL

> Wives' tale you mean.

CHRIS

> I don't. Could just as well be husbands'.

NOEL

> Owls. Not too keen on those fellas.

CHRIS

> Undo my arms. Just you undo them.
>
> *Pause.*
>
> Please.

NOEL

> You're learning. I just might. But, you be quiet. We have to wait.

CHRIS

> How long?

NOEL

> A bit longer. Won't be too long either.
>
> *Unties her hands. She picks up the doll.*

CHRIS

Do you have a girlfriend? Someone you care for?

Silence.

NOEL

None of your business.

CHRIS

But do you?

Pause.

Does she think you're a hero? Her hero? More fool her.

NOEL

It's dangerous to mock.

CHRIS

Does she love you? Do you tell her what you do? Do you have it off?

NOEL

You've got a dirty tongue. Be quiet.

CHRIS

Is she good in bed? In the sack?

NOEL

Just you shut up.

Turns the gun on her.

I ask the questions here.

CHRIS

Softly.

It's not like that. I don't know why I spoke that way. It's not the way I speak or think. Perhaps it's because I haven't any bullets. I've nothing but words to fire at you.

Pause.

It's not like that.

NOEL

It's not like that. No not a bit.

CHRIS

Very quietly.

What is it like then. For you?

NOEL

Oh - leave it alone.

Pause.

CHRIS

Alright.

Silence.

What's her name?

NOEL

>Dawn.

CHRIS

>Goodness.

NOEL

>No. That's not her name,
>
>*Silence.*

CHRIS

>Does she know…
>
>*Pause.*
>
>all this?

NOEL

>Will you be quiet. Leave me be.

CHRIS

>John is my best friend.

NOEL

>What a laugh.

CHRIS

>It's not a laugh.

NOEL

>You're a laugh. Just one big laugh. Think you

know all the answers, everything, so bloody smug.

CHRIS

Me, smug?

NOEL

You think you've got the handle on love. That it's yours. You own it. You think you know all about it, that you know and I don't. That people like me, don't. Young fellas like me, don't. Get stuffed. You know nothing... What do you know about? You risk nothing. Whatever you've done – it's nothing. I don't want my girl to be my best friend. She's... Oh, forget it - I don't speak of it. Some things are better not spoken of.

Silence.

You think you've got it all buttoned up, you and your tidy little family. Neat and tidy. As you say, it's not like that.

CHRIS

What's it like then? Since you know everything. How to solve everything. Even love.

Pause.

You don't know.

NOEL

> You don't know when to keep silent. I don't talk about my girlfriend. OK? She doesn't blab about me.

CHRIS

> Your dark lady.

NOEL

> I've read my Shakespeare. She's no man.

CHRIS

> What's your girlfriend's name?

NOEL

> I'll not tell you her name.
>
> *Silence.*
>
> Tell me about your brother.

CHRIS

> I love my brother.

NOEL

> Easy said.

CHRIS

> You love your dark lady.

NOEL

> Who's speaking about love?

Silence.

Tell me about your brother, what's he do?

CHRIS

> Why?

NOEL

> Just tell.

CHRIS

> There's nothing to tell. He lives and works, like civilised people do.

NOEL

> Civilised. I have one too, a brother, Jim, like yours.
>
> *Pause.*

CHRIS

> I don't expect my brother is anything like yours.

NOEL

> A brother's a brother. You know them and you don't know them.

CHRIS

> I know Jimmy. He's a lovely man. I don't see so much of him since he went to live in the North. He is an accountant in Coleraine. With a practice

in Belfast as well. I would like to see more of him. Why?

NOEL

It's well for some. Why did lovely brother Jimmy go to work in the North?

CHRIS

He was asked by his uncle to join his practice there.

NOEL

An uncle is it?

CHRIS

He's dead. Died last year. Car crash.

NOEL

That's the way it goes.

Pause.

Sorry for your trouble.

CHRIS

Thanks.

Pause.

So there's a human in you.

Pause.

You're still shaking.

NOEL

> And Charlie? Who's Charlie? What about Charlie?

CHRIS

> What about Charlie?

NOEL

> Where is he in the picture of your life?

CHRIS

> He's not. He's just not. I never see him. I never liked him, he was Jimmy's friend.

NOEL

> Why didn't you like him?

CHRIS

> Just the usual things as a child you know, he was older than Jimmy, and I was younger than them both. Charlie was a bit of a bully and a show-off, not bad but I was a softy, timid, and he knew it. And Jimmy was not able to stand up to him so I preferred it when he wasn't around. We had more fun.

NOEL

> You're not timid now.

CHRIS

> We toughen up. Have to.

NOEL

> What sort of fun? What did you do?

CHRIS

> You know kids' fun. Imagining different things. Adventures. Doing dares. Having secrets was so important. We had a secret sign.

NOEL

> What for?

CHRIS

> Oh, I don't think we knew, it was just ours. We had a password too.

NOEL

> Tell me.

CHRIS

> No. It was ours. Secret.

NOEL

> I want you to tell me.

CHRIS

> I won't.

NOEL grabs her, he is still shaking. CHRIS puts her hand on his as he is grabbing her.

CHRIS

You're hot, feverish, what's wrong with you?

NOEL

You will. Tell me. I can make you.

CHRIS

You tell me what you were doing when you put me in the car? You tell me where all those silage bags have gone and what was in them?

NOEL

Keep your nose out of what doesn't concern you. What's your maiden name?

CHRIS

My name is my own. My name doesn't concern you. I'll tell you nothing.

NOEL

Silly bitch.

Pause.

There's nothing in those bags but silage. What's the name of his firm, your brother's?

CHRIS

> Are you needing an accountant?

NOEL

> You never know, it might be his lucky day. Is it Hayden and Walsh? Jimmy Hayden?
>
> *CHRIS is very still. NOEL is still holding on to her. He begins to shake again.*

CHRIS

> What is wrong? You feel so hot. Have you a fever?

NOEL

> Leave me alone will you woman. I get this. It comes and goes.
>
> *He shakes violently and CHRIS holds him. He puts his head on her shoulder.*

CHRIS

> There, there. There, there.
>
> *Silence.*
>
> *The sound of heavy rain. Light fades down, then up again.*
>
> *Later.*

NOEL

>Why did you do it?

CHRIS

>What?

NOEL

>You know, woman. Don't play that innocent game on me.

CHRIS

>I'm not playing any game. This, here, is like some dreadful dream. Not a game I want to play.

NOEL

>I want to know.

CHRIS

>You can go on wanting.

NOEL

>Tell me. Tell me about it. I need to know.
>
>*Pause.*
>
>Please.

CHRIS

>You make me so angry.

NOEL

>Then why are you holding me?

CHRIS

> Because you're like a little animal in pain.

NOEL

> I'm not little. I'm the boss here.

CHRIS

> Are you?
>
> *NOEL waves the gun.*
>
> *With irony.*
>
> Oh yes, the gun. Bang, you're dead. Wonderful.

NOEL

> None of that, or it will be bang.

CHRIS

> I don't feel afraid of your gun. I don't feel a bloody thing about your gun. I feel dead tired.

NOEL

> My gun rules, baby. You have to listen. Whatever you spout on about, it's me with the gun that counts.

CHRIS

> I can die or be wounded. Dead, I'm someone else's problem. I'd be yours! Wounded, we survive these things.

NOEL

> How can a mother like you get rid of her child?
> It's unnatural, it's wicked.

CHRIS

> Stop it. Don't speak of what you haven't the
> vaguest, haven't a clue... Ignorant murdering
> little fool.

NOEL

> Keep a civil tongue in your head woman. That
> tongue of yours could land you in right trouble. I
> am asking you a question. Answer me.
>
> *Silence.*
>
> Tell me! I'm listening to you.
>
> *Silence.*

CHRIS

> *Quietly.*
>
> I had to make a decision. Such a hard decision,
> the hardest ever I will have to make. All this,
> this mad nightmare you're making here is partly
> nothing. Unreal, stupid. Nothing to do with me.
> Quite separate from me. You obey someone
> out there, a bit like God. You believe without
> doubting. What I have given up was a blueprint

of a child who might have been. A possibility of a child. Not a child. Happens all the time with miscarriages. All our griefs, so much grief.

NOEL

But why did you?

CHRIS

If I had another child it would reverse an operation that I had two years ago. They cannot do that operation again. It is not possible. My disability would return. I would have it for the rest of my life. That's it. That's all. It is absolutely not your business. I would be stuck with it forever. A life sentence. Maybe someone stronger than me could cope. I couldn't. I couldn't live with it, and still be a person. I know I can't, couldn't. So I've done what I did, had an abortion. That's it. That's all. There, I've said it. God I've said it. I never thought I'd say it. Why did I say it to you?

NOEL

What sort of problem, come on, what could be that bad?

CHRIS is silent.

You're just trying to justify yourself. That's

natural. But it doesn't change a thing.

CHRIS

Why do I bother? I can't talk to you. You're too thick.

NOEL

You're just guilty as hell, sweetheart, and won't face it.

CHRIS

Guilt? You talk to me about guilt? You? How dare you condemn and judge. Look at yourself and judge that. Ask yourself a few questions and answer them. Face them and really answer them.

Pause.

Should a child, raped by a father, have to bear that child? Would you like to be that child? A woman raped should bear a child - and love it?

That's being a saint. We can choose to be saints if we like. No law can demand us to be one.

NOEL

Sure you're full of talk. Doesn't mean a thing. Don't give me that crap.

CHRIS

What a fool I am to even try to talk to you. You

don't listen to anything you don't want to hear.
Why don't you think? You've got a brain, I hope.
It's not about being good. We took a choice.
We've our family to rear best we can. Please shut
up. I've had enough.

Silence.

St Dominic put a whole town to the sword, four
thousand men, women and children because they
refused to become Christians.

Pause.

And he's a saint! He is honoured. Bloody men.
Nothing changes.

NOEL

>Did he? Didn't know that. What an old fart. Had
>some muscle.

CHRIS

>You admire that? God almighty. Just like
>yourselves. Total hypocrites. I suppose that
>is what they call, a 'just war.' You can kill, to
>defend your faith and morals. As long as it's the
>right brand, see the whiteness, feel the width.
>You're the same. You kill for your daily bread…
>You give us this day, our daily death.

NOEL

> You're blaspheming...

CHRIS

> You little bossy boots with your gun. A bully like Charlie was. I'm not afraid of the Charlies of this world any more. Used to be. Now I don't seem to be anymore...

NOEL

> A just war, never heard of that one. What's that?

CHRIS

> Just a way of justifying violence. The bloody church's way. Oh, it all makes me so weary. All you all want is your own way. Don't you ever want peace?

NOEL

> I'm fighting for it. For justice, you silly bitch. For peace for Ireland. You don't know anything, living smug in Dublin. All nice and cosy. Think you're great, know everything. You don't know one real thing. You know nothing of the real world. You don't give a shag about us. As long as you're alright. You don't give a damn.

CHRIS

> Let me weep... Just weep.

NOEL

> Weep away.
>
> *Silence.*
>
> What if you're just making all that story up? Had it off with some fella. And you're just getting rid of a telltale. The result of your little bit on the side. All woman are at it now they have the pill. A man isn't safe any more. All this women's lib stuff, makes me puke.

CHRIS

> You snivelling brat, you think I was cheating on my husband? John knows what I'm doing, we decided it together and he is not with me because he is minding the children. Why do I bother talking to you? Waste of time.
>
> *Pushes him away.*
>
> Go on, go away, go away, play with your little boy's toys.
>
> *Turns from him.*

NOEL

> You haven't told me yet what your trouble is.

Pause.

This big disability you can't put up with. You're lying. Tell me. Tell me. Tell me. Sure you're just lying. Dirty bitch. I've no time at all for you. You deserve nothing.

Pause.

CHRIS

Listen. I've no need to explain to you. But you should begin to use your head and your heart, if you have one and I've seen precious little sign of that. But here's hoping. Here's to hope. And don't we need that? In this country, in this world? You and I need it. Listen. Then shut up.

Silence.

I'd be incontinent.

Silence.

NOEL

What's that mean?

CHRIS

For always. Till I die. Forever.

Silence.

I couldn't live with that.

Pause.

It means that I couldn't control my bladder.

Pause.

Ever.

NOEL

Bladder... Oh. You'd piss in your pants?

Begins to laugh.

CHRIS

Stop.

NOEL

Wet the bed?

CHRIS

Shut up.

NOEL

Piss your knickers?

CHRIS

Stop it. Don't. You're just vile.

NOEL

Sure that's nothing. What a laugh.

NOEL roars with laughter. CHRIS slaps him in the face. He jumps on her, pushes her to the ground and straddles her. Gun in between his straddling legs.

No woman ever raises a hand to me. You don't treat me that way. Right? Don't worry, baby, I don't screw other men's wives. I have standards.

Sees the blood stains.

I don't fuck bleeding cunts. I won't have your blood on me.

Cross fade to AUNT.

Scene Six

AUNT is on the phone.

AUNT

Is that you John? I'm glad I've got you. Are you well? Good, good. And the children? That's good. Well done...Well, that is what I'm phoning about. I wonder if Chris has phoned you? I see... Yes. Yes. Well, I agree with you it is late. I thought I should let you know she hadn't arrived yet. I am concerned. Not worried. Concerned... Yes a good idea, ring Pauline, she'll know when she left... Exactly... The news in the north is not that good... No it's quiet here. At the moment... No, we can't give it heed or we'd never do anything...

I think it would be. Could you get someone in at this hour? Well if you can, try, yes, do... No I'm quite alright. It's Chris, she's a very good driver and if anything had happened of course we would have heard. Take care. Bye, bye... Yes, give me a ring in half an hour, or as soon as you know if you can come... Bye, bye, John, speak again soon.

Pause. Replaces receiver.

We would have heard, wouldn't we Bono? Of course we would.

Scene Seven

Lights cross fade back to CHRIS and NOEL. Lights low. NOEL checks window, door, goes up into loft and looks out the window, comes back. Owls are heard. Lights up.

NOEL

I think, I'm...

Pause,

sorry for ye.

CHRIS looks at him.

Do you feel, OK? Are you, alright?

CHRIS

I'm as alright as you can be, held at gun point in the middle of the night, after... after... everything. And it's pissing rain. Yes. I'm fine. I'm just fine.

Silence.

NOEL

Tell me something. What was that password you had when you played here as kids then?

CHRIS

Oh goodness that! I can't remember.

NOEL

Of course you can. Go on. I'm one of the gang now.

CHRIS

No you're not. Never.

Pause.

You're the baddy. No, you're nothing.

NOEL

Well you have to have a baddy. And you're the goody. The goody-goody.

CHRIS

> No one could call me that. Charlie was the baddy, so we had one. Don't need you.

NOEL

> But you've got me. Tell me.

CHRIS

> What's this fever you've got?

NOEL

> Shut up about it. Might be brucellosis. Got it before. On my uncle's farm. Give me the password.

CHRIS

> Sounds silly now, Kuryakin. Our secret sign is somewhere,

NOEL

> Where? Show me?

CHRIS

> It was carved on a post I think. Jimmy carved it. It could protect us from aliens.
>
> *NOEL jumps up and looks.*

NOEL

> *Looking down the posts.*
>
> Can't see.

CHRIS

> I'd need to look.

NOEL

> Move, can't you.

CHRIS

> No.

NOEL

> I'll untie your legs, but no funny business mind.
> *Unties her legs.*

CHRIS

> There are ways I'd prefer to die than having my brains blown out by you.
>
> *They both look for the sign on the posts.*
>
> It's such a long time ago and I remember, but what I remember is different to what is here.

NOEL

> It always is.
>
> *Silence.*
>
> Why did you go though Belfast, to go to England,

to get your job done? Why not Dublin? No sense in it.

CHRIS

My parents can't know about it. Nor any of the family. They wouldn't understand. Wouldn't be able to take it. They are used to me staying a few days with Pauline. And with Auntie. They'll pass no remarks.

NOEL

Then we'd never have met?

CHRIS

Christ. Some disenchanted evening.

NOEL

What about Auntie?

CHRIS

She'll understand.

NOEL

Are you sure?

CHRIS

Yes. I'm sure about her.

Pause.

What are you sure about?

>   *NOEL does not answer.*
>
>   Why do you do this Noel?
>
>   *NOEL does not answer.*
>
>   How did you get into this... life... job, whatever you'd call it? I don't understand.

NOEL

>   Of course you don't. You with your cushy life.

CHRIS

>   Don't start that again.

NOEL

>   You're all just blind and ignorant you know nothing.
>
>   *CHRIS says nothing.*
>
>   Men broke into our house when I was four, my brothers were out, they killed my father, in front of me and my mother. My brothers could never get work. Listen woman, how do you know? What do you care? You only listen when you get hurt. My brothers joined. So did I. Later.
>
>   *Looks at CHRIS.*
>
>   You'd have done the same.
>
>   *She looks at him.*
>
>   You would.

Waits for her reply, gets none.

What a laugh.

CHRIS buries her head in her hands. NOEL gets up and walks away. Sits on a silage bale.

I'll tell you one thing. This way of making silage is great. My uncle uses it now. Expensive, he says, but well worth it. We went to his place in the summer to help with the hay when I was a kid. Good that. I can make a cock of hay. Then we made silage in big pits and drove the tractor over it. My uncle knew a man who would never feed his silage to his beasts until he'd tasted it himself. Said it was like good Christmas pudding.

CHRIS remains silent.

Used to hear the corncrake in the fields then. Not any more. It's gone. Gone, extinct.

Silence.

You didn't believe me that there is only silage in these bales did you?

CHRIS remains silent.

Well, let's take a look, I'll show you, no bother. Here you are. Inside here is good, clean, fodder for cattle. Never better.

NOEL straddles the silage bales and slices one with a knife. Out falls, head first, the bound and bloody dead body of CHARLIE. NOEL did not know CHARLIE was there. CHRIS is horror struck.

CHRIS

Charlie!

NOEL leaps to CHRIS and puts his hand over her mouth to stop her shouting.

NOEL

Fucking hell! What happened the poor sod?

CHRIS

Oh my God! Oh Jesus, Mary and Joseph!

NOEL

Who put the bastard there? Makes no sense.

CHRIS

He is dead? He is really dead? You're sure he's dead? There's no life left in him? Should we give him the kiss of life? Is there breath in him?

NOEL

Gets down by the body.

No girl. He's quite dead.

CHRIS

> *Sinks to her knees beside him.*
>
> Oh you had a dreadful death. A shameful death. Oh look at his knees!

NOEL

> They kneecapped him first.

CHRIS

> They shot him everywhere. Oh my God, why did they? Who are they?
>
> *Rounds on NOEL.*
>
> You killed him! You knew all the time. You rotten stinking bastard. You foul shit. You...

NOEL

> You're wrong woman. I know nothing of it. I don't like it.

CHRIS

> You knew Charlie!

NOEL

> Maybe I did, and maybe I didn't.

CHRIS

> How? Why? How did you?

NOEL

> This is the first time I set eyes on him.

CHRIS

> But you worked with him. He told you about the barn.
>
> *Silence.*
>
> He did, didn't he?

NOEL

> *Shrugs.*
>
> The boss decides.

CHRIS

> Why has this happened to him? What did he do?

NOEL

> Whatever he did, he must have been a naughty boy.

CHRIS

> You're bastards. The lot of you.
>
> *CHRIS sinks to her knees and mourns CHARLIE. NOEL is bleeped on the walkie-talkie and walks away and listens. Replies to CHRIS.*

NOEL

> End of our little jaunt now. I have things to do.

We'll be moving along soon, you and I, and our mutual friend here. Duty calls.

CHRIS

You make me sick.

NOEL

I'll just tie you up, if you don't mind.

CHRIS

I do mind, I'm going... I'm... I don't care...

NOEL

Don't spoil it all, baby, we were doing so nicely weren't we?

He ties her. She is sitting on the ground by CHARLIE's body. NOEL goes to the upper level and speaks on the walkie-talkie, checks out the window. Puts maps and papers in a briefcase. Makes signals, packs a bag etc., getting ready for his evacuation. A police siren is heard.

Lights go down slowly on NOEL in the loft section gradually to blackout during the following prayer and conversation with CHARLIE and CHRIS. The audience should still be aware of NOEL at his business.

CHRIS

>Hail holy Queen, Mother of Mercy.

>*NOEL speaks on the walkie-talkie.*

NOEL

>Finished.

CHRIS

>Our life, our sweetness, and our hope.

>To thee do we cry, poor banished children of Eve.

NOEL

>Fifteen, twenty minutes. That should do it.

CHRIS

>To thee do we send up our sighs...

NOEL

>Found him. Thanks for telling me.

>*Pause.*

>She is.

CHRIS

>...mourning and weeping in this veil of tears.

NOEL

>Yes.

>*Pause.*

>I understand. Yes. Over and out.

CHRIS

> Turn then most gracious Advocate, thine eyes
> of mercy towards us. And after this our exile...
> Oh clement, oh loving, oh sweet virgin Mary,
> pray for us. Oh holy Mother of God, that we may
> be made worthy of the promises, worthy of the
> promises, worthy, made worthy...

> *During this prayer, we go into a 'resurrection' or dream sequence. CHARLIE becomes alive and CHRIS and he talk. CHARLIE goes and unties CHRIS's bonds. CHARLIE gets up cheerfully.*

CHARLIE

> Hi Chris!

CHRIS

> Charlie!

CHARLIE

> Great to see you. Great. Been ages. How are you? You look great. How are the kids? John? Oh God, remember this place? The times we had. Really great. Just the same. Nothing changes.

CHRIS

> How... are you Charlie? Oh Charlie!

CHARLIE

> Never better. A.1. In the pink, as they say. Do you know I don't think I've seen you since your wedding. Can you believe it! That's one for the books. Such old friends as us. Old friends are the best, as they say. I must say you've turned out one hell of a smashing looking woman. Uurrgh. John knew how to pick 'em. Messed up there didn't I?
>
> *Laughs.*
>
> Still I'm not the marrying type. But if you fancy a little nookie on the side. I'm your man.

CHRIS

> What a kind offer...

CHARLIE

> Holy shit, it all comes back to me, your wedding. Wonder you didn't throw me out. Went a bit over board on the booze. Smashing day. Just great. You looked great. John looked great. Jimmy, do you see old Jimmy at all, Chrissy? Jimmy was the Best Man wasn't he? Do I remember rightly? I was all over your old auntie, she's a lovely woman. Great. I did do well on the booze though and sang that song that had all the aunties and

your Mammy and Daddy going white at the gills. God it was smashing. Remember?

CHRIS

Yes, Charlie, I do.

CHARLIE

It was great, if I ever get married I'll have a wedding like yours. You're the expert. But I've missed my chance with the best bride in the world, haven't I now?

CHRIS

You have.

CHARLIE

Can't win 'em all, that's what I say. I haven't done too badly, here and there.

CHRIS

What do you do Charlie?

CHARLIE

Oh, a bit of this, a bit of that. Trading, you know, here and there. Done quite well for myself. Now and again. If I kept away from the booze and the horses I'd be a rich man, but you know me. I like a good time. I like company. I put people first, like friends, like you and me and Jimmy. That's important, I tell you for nothing, that is very important in my life.

CHRIS

Charlie, have you seen Jimmy lately?

CHARLIE

Lord yes. See a lot of him. All the time, well on and off, you know how it is, time flies...

CHRIS

How is he? When did you last see him?

CHARLIE

Only the other day, when was it? He's just fine, great. Knows a thing or two does our Jimmy. Sound man.

CHRIS

I see him so little now.

CHARLIE

You were always the soft one. Liked you for that. Loved your dolly so you did.

CHRIS

When do you see Jimmy?

CHARLIE

Well, now and again, speak on the phone, give

him a tinkle. Keep in touch. I see him at the
club when I drop in for a pint, playing squash.
Jimmy's a brilliant player. Fast and hard. Keeps
in trim does our Jim. There, I'm a poet. Hidden
talents in your old Charlie.

CHRIS

You've kept good mates, you and Jimmy?

Pause.

Do you ever work for Jimmy, Charlie?

CHARLIE

Strictly confidentially, between you and me,
now and again he puts the odd little job my way.
Keep it under your hat and all that, the tax man
cometh, you know the sort of thing. Has contacts
does our Jimmy. He's a good operator, have to
hand it too him. He's a cute hoor.

CHRIS

What sort of job would you do for him, Charlie?
Jimmy's an accountant, you're not exactly in that
area are you?

CHARLIE

You could say that, you could, and you'd be
right. But you know how it is, now and again we

all need someone to deal with little things that come up. Jimmy has some big deals going on, I wouldn't know the half of it.

Pause.

As if this is a new idea.

You and John should ask him down some time. I am sure he'd love to have a good old heart-to-heart with his little sister.

CHRIS

Do you think I haven't?

CHARLIE

Not really listening and carrying on.

I'm sure he'd really love that Chris, get down to dear old Dublin. You should ask him. You really should. Just love to see you, John and the kids, he'd just love that. My goodness they must be big now?

CHRIS

Charlie, what's happened? You, now, what? Tell me, I... explain... all this. Oh Charlie.

CHARLIE

This?

Looks at himself.

Pissed off about it, to tell the truth. Sorry about the language. Not a nice way to treat a friend. There you are, there are some very untrustworthy people about.

CHRIS

Are you... dead?

CHARLIE

Me? Dead? Jesus! What a thought. Things like that don't happen to Charlie. No. No. It's not like that at all, at all. I... this is... just a temporary inconvenience.

Pause.

Bumped me off before I got my money - the bastards. Ah, that's the way, the way of this bloody world. Didn't do it very nicely either. Painful. Bloody botched job. Why should something like this happen to me, I ask you? Why me?

CHRIS

I suppose you could say it's a chance to see how the other half lives.

Laughs. Silence.

CHARLIE

> Didn't expect to see me here, did you? To tell you the honest truth I didn't expect to be here either. This old place, this old barn where we used to play, you, me and Jimmy. Funny isn't it? Who'd have thought we'd meet here of all places?

Goes to the side of the barn.

> There, Jimmy and I carved that. Remember this? Some old sign we thought important. Funny things kids get up to. Jimmy's penknife broke.

CHRIS

> You remember it?

CHARLIE moves over to the side of the barn and gives it a kick with his foot.

CHARLIE

> See, there you are. Old Charlie never forgets.

CHRIS

> You're right. It is there.

CHARLIE

> Of course it's there. I told you it was there.

CHRIS

> To protect us against the aliens.

CHARLIE

What's that?

CHRIS

To protect us.

CHARLIE

I didn't remember the sign was for that. Funny that. I'm good at remembering things. Known for his good memory is old Charlie. Are you sure that's what it was for? Very funny that. It did protect us didn't it? They didn't get us. We got them though. Great games. Great times. And great to see you looking so smashing. Just smashing. I loved those times. Very special they are to me. Our little group. You, me and Jimmy. I really felt I belonged. Never felt I belonged like that anywhere else in my whole life. Would you credit that now? Never. We were close. Good mates. Good it was. Real good. They were happy, happy times. Happy, happy times....

CHARLIE gets up and goes as if in a dream to where he fell out of the bag. Ties CHRIS up and then slowly falls back to death. Light may change for this. NOEL has finished his work and comes down. He begins the evacuation. Drags

CHARLIE's body towards the car, opens the boot and begins to haul the body up into it.

CHRIS

>Stop. Where are you taking him?
>
>*NOEL ignores her.*
>
>Don't do that. He's a person. Give him respect. Undo me, I can help.
>
>*Silence from NOEL.*
>
>I could help, let me, please.
>
>*NOEL does not react and folds CHARLIE roughly into the boot space.*

NOEL

>*Was* a person, baby. Now just meat...

CHRIS

>May he rest in peace.

NOEL

>Not our problem. He rests... in pieces.

CHRIS

>May the soul of the faithful departed-

NOEL

>He's departed, quite faithfully...

CHRIS

> -rest in peace.

NOEL

> Get moving. No time to hang around. Job's done. Here. Almost.

CHRIS

> Lord have mercy.

NOEL

> He's in his coffin.
>
> *Laughs. Bangs the lid of the boot.*

CHRIS

> Christ have mercy.

NOEL

> He'll have a good big send off. He's going to go up like the Vikings.

CHRIS

> Lord have mercy.

NOEL

> Stop that. Get in the car.

CHRIS

> Christ have mercy.

NOEL

> *Roughtly tries to put CHRIS in the passenger seat. CHRIS resists.*

CHRIS

> Stop it. I'm not going anywhere with you. What are you doing with Charlie?

NOEL

> None of your business, baby. Your friend Charlie has a nice little cremation waiting for him. Not too far from here either. And you-

CHRIS

> I'm not going with you.

NOEL

> Now who's the foolish woman?

CHRIS

> Do you know my brother Jimmy?

NOEL

> *Pause.*
>
> If I know a Jimmy or two how would I know if one of them was your brother?

CHRIS

> You would. Tell me?

NOEL

> You talk too much and think too little. And this isn't choosing time for you, girl. What would be nicer than a little jaunt in the car? How about a nice cup of tea with Auntie?
>
> *Blackout. Sound of car starting. The car lights up into the eyes of the audience. Blackout.*

Scene Eight

Dark. The sound of heavy rain. Light up on AUNT and CHRIS in AUNT's house. They are holding each other.

AUNT

> Chris, Chris, allanah. Are you hurt?

CHRIS

> I'm alright. I think I'm alright. I don't feel anything. I seem to be in one piece. The night, the long night. Is there a glimmer of morning yet?

AUNT

> Not yet. It will come.

CHRIS

> We need the light. The light shrinks the nightmare. Nothing is safe. But in the light it is better than in the dark.

AUNT

> Put this round you.
>
> *Puts a rug around her.*

CHRIS

> I fought a battle all night. I was a sort of soldier. I don't know if I won or not. I don't know.

AUNT

> You'll be alright, love. We will. Everything will be alright.

CHRIS

> Of course I didn't win. It is not about winning at all.

AUNT

> You'll be fine. You need to rest.

CHRIS

> I don't know. The fire is good. I can't feel its warmth.

AUNT

> Come closer. Sit closer. Move, Bono.

CHRIS

> That's good.
>
> *Pause.*
>
> I don't know if there is any good anywhere.

AUNT

> Come, I'll put you to bed.

CHRIS

> Anywhere at all in the world. Do you think there is any?
>
> *They react as if hearing Bono bark.*
>
> Bono barked! Someone might be there. Someone might be outside.

AUNT

> Don't worry. She's excited. All this disturbance. I'll look. Don't worry.

CHRIS

> Oh, don't look! Stay in. Stay here. Wait for dawn.

AUNT

> Just you rest. I'll stay.

CHRIS

> Nowhere is safe. Nothing. Anywhere. Charlie's dead. He's all... dead.

AUNT

> You told me love. You're alive. That's what counts.

CHRIS

> I expected to be dead.
>
> *Pause.*
>
> And I'm not dead. Yet.

AUNT

> You're alive, my love. Thank God. Thank God.

CHRIS

> This grief, my grief, I'm carrying all the grief in the world.

AUNT

> Sit there while I make us something hot.
>
> *She moves to the side to prepare a hot drink. She is as if off-stage, out of the spot, in the dark.*

CHRIS

> It's too heavy. Too heavy for me. It's too heavy for all of us.

AUNT

> *From the dark.*

> I phoned John. John is on his way now.

CHRIS

> I don't think John should come here. I think John should stay away. This is not the place for John.
>
> *Silence.*
>
> Is Jimmy alright? Do you think? I'm afraid to think about that. That seems a very dark place to think about.
>
> *Silence.*
>
> Auntie, tell me, what do you think? What you think about Jimmy?

AUNT

> Don't bother yourself about Jimmy. Jimmy's fine. Why wouldn't he be?
>
> *NOEL appears silently behind CHRIS, masked and with a gun. AUNT appears fractionally after NOEL, unseen by him and knocks the gun from his hand. She swiftly picks the gun up and turns it on him.*
>
> Go. Now. Get out fast.
>
> *NOEL turns.*

CHRIS

>Noel.

>*He stops.*

>Why did you come back? You could have killed me any time, why let me come here and... Who's your boss? Is it Jimmy?

NOEL

>Curiosity killed the cat. That would be telling, baby. As I said there are lots of Jims in this world. You'd better ask Kuryakin. So long. See yer. I'll be back.

>*He departs. AUNT moves after him and raises the gun to shoot. CHRIS stops her.*

CHRIS

>Don't. Stop.

>*Silence.*

>*CHRIS takes the gun from her aunt.*

>Leave that game to them.

>*They lean against each other.*

>We've our lives to be getting on with.

>*Pause.*

AUNT

> As best we can.

CHRIS

> If we can.

AUNT

> Look. There. The first light, the dawn is coming at last. The light is with us.
>
> *Pause.*
>
> I think I can hear the birds.
>
> *The women hold each other. A slight pale light of dawn appears. A vixen's cry is heard. The rain continues.*

www.ingramcontent.com/pod-product-compliance
Lightning Source LLC
Chambersburg PA
CBHW072051290426
44110CB00014B/1632